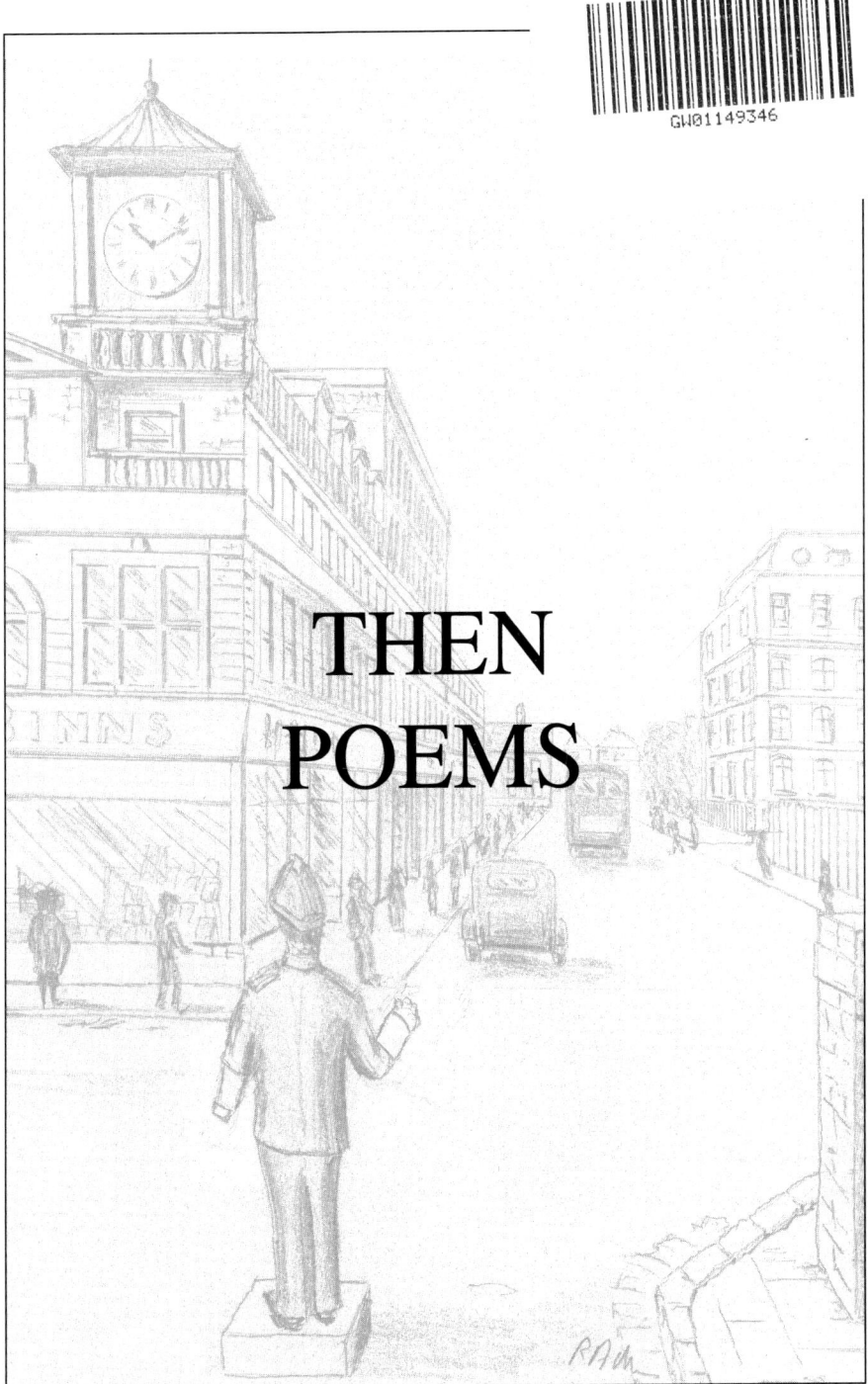

THEN POEMS

SEATON BATHS

Epilogue as a Prologue

It's not there now and there's nothing much to see
As you drive along the front where the Baths used to be,
Many years have passed since they knocked the old place down
A lot of locals felt it was an asset to the town.

I was one of many kids from Elwick Road School
Who learnt to doggie paddle in that ancient pool,
The Bus would arrive to take us for our weekly swim
As the teacher lined us up and bid us follow him.

We didn't have big sports bags, or all the fancy kit
A towel and a cossie, which very rarely fit,
There always was a danger when diving from a height
Of cossie flying down your legs, t'was not a pretty sight.

Along the Seaton front with that smell in the air
It was probably from the Steelworks, but no one seemed to care,
Our destination nearing, excitement and the fuss
As we fought with other kids to be the first one off the Bus.

Once inside the building, the smell it stung your nose
A mixture of disinfectant and piles of sweaty clothes,
The Superintendent stood there, a man of power and might
"Boys to the left" He shouted, "Girls to the right".

Equality for the sex's, you must be joking mate
For when we talk of changing rooms, the girls came out first rate,
The lads stripped off beside the Pool, with clammy freezing feet
Their modesty protected by a big tarpaulin sheet.

They had a funny method of teaching you to swim
By modern safety standards it really was quite grim,
Around ones skinny middle, was tied a sturdy rope
The face of the condemned, showed an utter lack of hope.

Poems *of* Hartlepool

THEN & NOW

Verse and Illustrations

by
Dik Milner

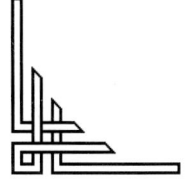

© **Dik Milner 2002**
Published by Printability Publishing Ltd. on behalf of Dik Milner.

Printed by Atkinson Print,
10/11 Lower Church Street, Hartlepool TS24 7DJ
Tel: 01429 267849   Fax: 01429 865416
ISDN No. 01429 894231   E-mail: enquiries@atkinsonprint.co.uk
www.atkinsonprint.co.uk

ISBN No. 1 872239 38 2
First Edition October 2002
Second Edition September 2007

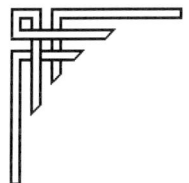

DEDICATED TO

CAROL, ANTHONY & TIMOTHY

Because they listened

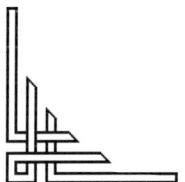

Foreword

Having resided for over half a century within the boundaries of the HARTLEPOOLS, I have felt the need during recent years to record in a somewhat simple way, a number of the many impressions the local area has made upon me.

The material within this edition has been divided by time. The 'THEN' poems are associated with early memories of the Town from childhood days and the 'NOW' poems reflect a more recent or topical view. I have written with the intention of eliminating wherever possible, unnecessary words or superfluous phrases, however some of the later poems, due to their subject content, do carry a certain licence in this respect.

I trust that the contents of this book may awaken happy memories in certain reader's minds and possibly bring amusement to others who may relate in some way to the instances and situations portrayed.

Dik Milner

CONTENTS

THEN POEMS

Seaton Baths	5
Elephant Rock	7
Back Yard Heroes	9
Wagga Moon	11
Seacoal	13
Slag Bank	17
Trolley Buses	19
Divvy	21
Our Bogie	22
Circus Monkey	25
Leaving School	27
Lynn Street on a Saturday	29
Cinema (That never was)	31
Blue Buses	33
Tattie Picken	35
Shop at Binns	37
Policeman at Binns Corner	40
Six of the Best	41

NOW POEMS

Cleveland R.I.P.	43
Iron Horse	45.
Eye of the Night	47
Milkman	49
Ode to Cable TV	51
Old Man and the Breakwater	53
Marina	55
Growing Old in Hartlepool	57
The Wesley	59
On the Dole Again	61
Power Station	63
Seagulls	65
Whatever Happened to Sunday	67
Steelworks Bridge	69
Rubbish	71

They walked you to the deep end and stood you near the side
"Don't worry son, its very safe, no one's ever died",
So leaping in the water, abandoning fear and doubt
And praying very earnestly, please someone pull me out.

The Pool was pure Sea Water, as salty as could be
It put a redness around the eyes, of the other swimmers and me,
And then there was the chlorine to keep the germs at bay
It also bleached your face white, as it washed the colour away.

Certificates were given if you passed a certain test
Like retrieving a rubber brick, whils't wearing pants and vest,
As the brick sank in the deep end, you silently prayed that fate
Would guide its course away, from that scary outlet grate.

I'm sure there are still many, who really miss that place
Who often came home with a chlorine blasted face,
So as you swim in the Mill House, please spare a thought
To the rope and to the deep end, in the Baths where you were taught.

ELEPHANT ROCK

It didn't resemble an Elephant
As you looked from over the wall,
No sign of a trunk or flapping ears
Although it looked quite tall.
But did that really matter
To adventurers of twelve years old,
Elephant Rock was what it was
Or so the story's told.
Apparently it looked the part
In our Grandparents day,
But tide and wind had done their part
And worn its shape away.
But to a gang of Westies
Who'd come here for the day,
The site was sacred in our eyes
We had many games to play.
It could be Treasure Island
Washed by a distant sea,
With hordes of cut-throat pirates
Attacking the gang and me.
Or maybe a Wizards Castle
Perched on a wooded hill,
With fire breathing Dragons
Prowling for the kill.
Hours of happy fun were spent
Upon those sandstone rocks,
And as the tide came rushing in
Off came the shoes and socks.
We'd change into our swimmies
And bravely paddle out,
Into the crashing breakers
With looks of fear and doubt.
Packed lunches were a luxury
We never really had,
A bottle of water and midget gems
Seemed enough for a growing lad.

Enthusiasm finally left us
As the tide ebbed slowly down,
So then we'd all get ready
For the journey back to town.
Another Adventure over
Having bid each one farewell,
Then hurrying home to mother
Each with his tale to tell.
With dinners in our tummies
Then into bed we rolled,
But very often ended up
With sneezes, coughs and colds.
And as we drifted nearer
Towards that land of nod,
We quietly whispered out a prayer
And gave our thanks to GOD.

BACK YARD HEROES

Now in the Nineteen Forties, having won the second world war
When many men still wondered what the fighting had been for,
Those times were really hard and the money it was short
For now the enemy had changed and it was poverty they fought.

But slowly life got better as the Forties passed away
Employment was increasing and with it peoples pay,
Families took short holidays, couples went out for meals
Then suddenly it started, everyone wanted wheels.

Now a lot of men they took the plunge and bought a motor car
Like little Fords and Austins, which took them near and far,
Personal independence had really come at last
The sound of Horse and Cart became an echo of the past.

But some could not afford the four wheeled transport mode
They needed something cheaper to get out on the road,
The BSA's the Norton's the Vincent's and the like
Their object of desire was the British Motorbike.

So the flat cap and the goggles became a common sight
As man and Iron Horses rode out, like Knights off to a fight,
Warfare was not intended as they cruised about the place
For the Battle with the Beastie put the grin upon their face.

The Rider became the mechanic of his two wheeled trusty steed
With brakes and tappets to adjust and a carburettor to bleed.
Changing oil and spark plugs, ignition advance retard
And the venue for this work, was in his very own Back Yard.

Yes, most Folk lived in terraced streets all those years ago
With real coal fires aburning and the good old bedroom poe,
So the Back Yards proved very handy, for a man and his machine
He could mess about for hours on end, just to keep it clean.

The house always stunk of petrol, there was oil on the kitchen floor
And usually a couple of other blokes, standing at the Back Street door,
Wives would shout "ya dinners ready, aren't ya finished yet"?
Followed by the usual reply of, "I won't be a minute pet".

But life just didn't stay the same, the Birds and Bees you see
That Stork would land and visit them, so families grew to three,
Different types of wheels appeared, Pushchairs, Prams the like
So now the Sword of Damocles, hung over the Hero's Bike

But some men built a little car and stuck it on the side
So Mam and Dad and all the kids could go out for a ride,
The Fathers felt quite proud as they cruised along the road
With funny hand signals, from the post war highway code.

Younger men had different thoughts and other Bikes in mind
They wanted more performance, the faster revving kind,
The Sixties were upon us, Mini Skirts and the Coffee Bar
Lads dreamed of the Triumph Bonnerville or the BSA Gold Star.

Have all these Back Yard Heroes, disappeared with time?
The men with oily faces, their fingers thick with grime,
Some rode combinations with the wife and kids on board
Just happy to be together, as down your street they roared.

So if on some occasion you spot a British Bike
Remember the noise emitted by Thunderbirds and the like,
And how the old Back Streets seem much quieter today
For the winds of time have carried those exhaust notes far away.

The Author aged 16 years astride a James 225cc Colonel
Location: An Osborne Road Back Yard 1959

WAGGA MOON

Laying in my bed at night, laying very still
Eyes wide open, staring hard, wondering if it will,
Light the sky from east to west with the colour red,
It comes and goes so very quick like thoughts within my head.

The sky looks dark and scary, I shiver in my room.
And clouds pass by so quickly like Harbingers of Doom,
The curtains should be closed now, I dare not leave my bed,
My mind is full of Ghostlike things the living and the dead.

    Wagga Moon, Wagga Moon
    Burning in the Night,
    Wagga Moon, Wagga Moon
    Let me see your light.

My eyelids start to droop now, Sandman is on his way
Memories quickly fading of happenings today,
I catch a glimpse of Moonlight above the blackened cloud,
But moments later gone again as if within a shroud.

Then suddenly the Sky lights up, a brightness comes at last
I'm wide awake, then out of bed all fear is in the past,
Small fingers on the window sill as through the glass I stare,
No more dark or scary Sky, there's Magic in the air.

    Wagga Moon, Wagga Moon
    Burning in the Night,
    Wagga Moon, Wagga Moon
    Let me see your light.

It's come at last. I knew it would, It never lets me down
That special Light that shines at night and captivates our Town.
The clouds are full of colour like the dawning of the day
I watch with silent wonder as it's beauty fades away.

I'm back inside my bed again and settled for the night
No scary thoughts of Ghosties now I've seen my magic light
Childlike sleep takes over to banish every care
My special light may shine again but I'll never know it's there.

       Wagga Moon, Wagga Moon
       Burning in the Night,
       Wagga Moon, Wagga Moon
       Let me see your light.

SEACOAL

Prologue.

He blows his nose on a piece of rag
And shouts again two bob a bag,
His barrow trundles down the street
We hear the pacing of his feet.

Once again his mournful cry
For any person who wants to buy,
At last he passes on his way
But he'll be back another day.

The North Sea pounds our Eastern shore
Relentless waves of natures might,
How wonderful to watch those tides
That ebb and flow each day and night.

Sweet influence of the Moon takes hold
And draws back water from the land,
The Beach grows larger all the while
Exposing rocks and miles of sand.

Yet other eyes have watched this sight
As Moon and tide their cycle run,
These watchers come out any time
At midnight hour or morning sun.

Patiently they sit and wait
These men in lorries from the town,
With weathered face, their eyes alert
They closely watch the sea go down.

Others too, have come today
Some on bikes and some with carts,
Like the other men they also have
A common purpose in their hearts.

The tide is down, the men move out
There's a harvest to be reaped,
Each knows his task, no need to ask
Get the seacoal raked and heaped.

Yes, the cause of all this industry
Are the dark stains everywhere,
The sea has left its tidemark
And the men fight for their share.

They worked in gangs, the men with trucks
It took some power and might,
To shovel all that seacoal
Up to lorry's height.

So loaded up to the limit
The truck sets off at a crawl,
It seems like mission impossible
To get off the beach at all.

But the driver does his thing once more
And the lorry reaches the road,
Cruising back to the town again
For the place to weigh the load.

Those entrepreneurs of Hartlepool
Doing their bit for the nation,
Helping to keep the boilers alight
At North Tees Power Station.

But, remember too those other men
Who came here for the coal,
For many families found it hard
Existing on the dole.

This free fuel warmed many a home
Through a chilly winters night,
For banked on top of normal coal
It kept those fires alight.

Yet others filled their little carts
And to the town they walked,
Shouting up and down the street
As bags of fuel they hawked.

Two bob a bag was quite a sum
In Nineteen Fifty Five,
Although many had work, the pay was low
It was a struggle to survive.

Epilogue

No more that seacoal seller
With barrow and shuffling feet,
Two bob a bag, two bob a bag
Was the echo down our street.

SLAG BANK

My father was in Dads Army
Or the Home Guard by it's right name,
And often he was out all night
Playing at the Soldiers game.

They didn't have Captain Mainwaring
But another of similar rank,
And they did some of their training
On the Brenda Road Slag Bank.

A kind of man made plateau
On the southern side of town,
A result of the old steelworks
And the ore they melted down.

For many a year it stood there
Hot furnaces making it glow,
As load after load from containers
Spewed out a molten flow.

As time passed by the Steelworks
Finally ground to a halt,
The Government blamed recession
But we know who was at fault.

Yes, the Slag Bank took its rest then
And the white larva ceased to flow,
No more that famous WAGGA MOON
With its eerie night time glow.

As time rolled on that ugly hill
Played host to another force,
It started turning shades of green
As nature took its course.

No more that local landmark
Where Dads Army used to fight,
And chase pretendy Germans
Up and down its height.

The machines were called to action
For a decision was made one day,
So scrapers and lorries attacked it
and hauled the bank away.

Epilogue.

So if you pass down Brenda Road
Please stop and take in the view,
For you'll see the Slag Bank still exists
To the east of B & Q.

TROLLEY BUSES

Scary things those buses
They never made much noise,
Travelling along the road
Like big red dinky toys.

They had strange poles upon their roofs
Like feelers on a bee,
I was only very small
They seemed so big to me.

The buses came up Church Street
For journeys through the Town,
And when they reached Binns corner
Sometimes they would break down.

The driver off the bus would leap
And look up to the sky,
He'd shake his head and stamp his feet
"The poles come off", he'd cry.

But problems soon got sorted out
The pole fixed back in place,
So off the trolley bus went again
With a smile on the driver's face.

It's a pity they stopped those buses
Yes, it's sad they've had their day,
For it was always good to travel round
In such a quiet and peaceful way.

THE DIVVY

One Three Seven Eight Six
Those numbers that stuck in your head,
As you ran down the street to the Co-op
For potatoes and a loaf of brown bread.
"Remember to give them the number"
Said your mam, as you shot out the door,
"Make sure they write it down now"
She added, whilst dusting the floor.

"One Three Seven Eight Six"
You said to the girl at the till,
And watched her very carefully
As she jotted them down on the bill.
Then clutching your purchases tightly
All messages done for the day,
You hurried back home to your mother
And hoped you could go out to play.

One Three Seven Eight Six
A Co-operative profit share,
And it all added up to a dividend
That was paid at the end of the year.
Yes, that bonus proved very handy
Solving many a financial fix,
And as long as I live I'll remember
One Three Seven Eight Six.

OUR BOGIE

A set of pram wheels from a scrapyard
Plus two strong pieces of wood,
And a big nut and bolt if you could find one,
Then your bogie was starting to look good.

I'd better explain from the beginning
And introduce those kids in my gang,
There was my very best mate Mad Mickey
Ginger Pete, and a lad named Wang.

We'd seen other kids with a bogie
So decided we'd have one as well,
"My Dad knows a man at the scrapyard"
Said Pete, who you always could smell.

Mad Mickey said, he'd get all the timber
"But you might find it painted bright red",
I suddenly knew where he'd get it
Next door had the same colour shed.

"We can build it in our back yard"
Said Wang, with a smile on his face,
"My Dads got some tools and a workshop"
We all agreed, it seemed the right place.

Straight after school the next Friday
Just wanting to get on with the job,
We arrived at Kindon's scrap yard
And bought an old pram for two bob.

Saturday morning proved quite hectic
But we did what needed to be done,
And with blood ousing out of elastoplasts
We were ready for some carting fun.

The bogie was tested in the back street
Each took their turn on the cart,
Mad Mickey hit a dog that was sleeping
When the steering bolt fell apart.

Pete said "We need somewhere slopey"
"To get up some speed, you know",
It was Wang who came up with the answer
"The Burn Valley is the place to go".

Up Elwick Road we all wandered
Then left through the Burn Valley gates,
"It looks a bit steep", I uttered
Glancing across at my mates.

We all took our turns on the Bogie
Thundering down the slope,
Then a slight right turn at the bottom
As you pulled like mad on the rope.

Yes, the end of that slope was dicey
As you steered like a nervous wreck,
Cos if you didn't make it across the bridge
You would end up in the beck.

Mad Mickey was not very happy
He wanted more speed you see,
As he jumped on the cart he shouted
"Come on, push like mad you three".

We really gave him a send off
As down the path he sped,
"I really don't think he'll make it"
Said Pete, with a shake of his head.

We stood there in silent wonder
I had visions of a hospital bed,
Mickey missed the bridge by inches
"Ah Soo" Wang quietly said.

It looked like he was going to make it
Then he went into a sideways slew,
Mick and the cart shot up in the air
Then disappeared from view.

Racing down the path then
We stopped at the side of the beck,
Our precious cart was a write off
Pete said "Oh flipping heck"

We all stared down at Mad Mickey
As he swam back to the side,
I said "Have you seen the state of our Bogie"
"That's the last time you have a ride"

That was the first of many Bogies
Made by the gang and me,
But in future, when in the Burn Valley
We drove very carefully.

Epilogue

That long straight path has gone now
It's full of twists and turns,
To safeguard pram pushing mothers
Out walking with their bairns.

CIRCUS MONKEY

I am a little Monkey and the Circus is my life,
I belong to Rene' the ringmaster and his fat German wife.
We're back in the North East and just got off the Train
At Hartlepool railway station oh, life can be a pain.

I run around and chatter while the animals get in line,
I pull faces at the tigers, all the children think I'm fine,
When everybody's ready it's across the Town we're bound,
Heading up to Rift House and the Recreation Ground.

There's always crowds of people on the streets of the Town,
Watching all the novelties, the man on stilts, the clown,
I like to watch the children as they laugh and clap their hands,
And point to all these creatures from far and distant lands.

Eventually we get there, then the work it really starts,
Everyone has a job to do emptying all the carts,
The Big Top needs erecting all the Animals want their tea,
Its all been too exciting for a Little Monkey like me.

So I find a broken bale of straw and lay down for a rest,
It's only a matter of seconds and I'm snoring in my nest,
My mind is starting to wander, eating peanuts covered in cream,
Then suddenly it's changing to this horrible scary dream.

I'm shipwrecked on this coastline all hungry cold and wet,
The boat it was a French one, I was the Captains pet,
These crowds of Hartlepool people, on the shore to welcome me,
They don't seem very happy as they dunk me in the sea.

Then suddenly things turn nasty, there's a rope around my neck,
No one seems to understand I've swum here from a wreck,
Running madly away from them, I fight with tooth and claw,
Then with a start, I'm awake again, in my little bed of straw.

The first night, its all over, Rene' seems a happy man
He's counting all the takings in his Circus caravan
I'm glad I'm not that Monkey, that many years before
Found that rope around his neck upon that headland shore.

LEAVING SCHOOL – STARTING WORK

Nineteen Fifty Eight was the year that I left school
And jobs they were aplenty in our town of Hartlepool,
The shipyard and the steelworks, many hundreds did employ
Obtaining work proved easy for a fifteen year old boy.

I started with the Council at their depot in Green Street
And the foreman electrician was the man I had to meet,
He just looked down at me and commented on my size
"you're not very big" he said, and stared into my eyes.

A state I must have looked in brand new bib and brace
Just over five feet tall, with a pale unweathered face,
My mother had worked wonders to adjust my working kit
But with the crutch around my knees, it seemed a funny fit.

The other apprentice electricians were older and bigger than me
So I did menial tasks, like sweeping up or making the tea,
Two pound two shilling and sixpence, that was my weekly wage
A reasonable amount of money for a person of my age.

Workmen seemed much happier then, in those by-gone days
Life still had its problems, but in not so many ways,
Apprentices got a thumping, if they stepped out of line
But do the job correctly and everything was fine.

The jobs were very varied and you worked all over town
But there always was a place that really got you down,
I'd be sent to the slaughter house, to mend something that was wrong
There'd be animals running everywhere and that stomach churning pong.

House repairs at Owton Manor and you walked there I might add
All good healthy exercise for a young and growing lad,
If the tenant happened to be out, we'd leave a calling card
Then really take our time as we walked back to the yard.

A year I spent on the Council and made good mates as well
They've gone their separate ways now, too many here to tell,
There was Ces of Storm Electrics, who now has a little store
Dave Casey was another, and many, many, more.

At the ripe old age of sixteen, I joined the Electricity Board
There was vans to ride about in, and a wage that suddenly soared,
Three Pounds Ten Shillings and Six Pence, what a monetary perk
Yet I missed that place in Green Street, where I had started work.

Epilogue

If someone is not sure where Green Street used to be
Arrive at Tesco roundabout, then Mac-Donalds you will see,
This burger bar now occupies the spot in Hartlepool
Where I started work, the day after leaving school.

LYNN STREET – On a Saturday

People, People everywhere
  On either side of the street,
The sound of double deckers
  The tramp, tramp, tramp, of feet,
Where have they all come from?
  What is there to see?
Lynn Street on a Saturday
  Seemed the place you had to be.

When the pavements got too crowded
  They'd just walk out on the road,
Which made it that much harder
  For those buses with a full load,
The drivers would blast their horns
  And steer with all their skill,
They didn't knock anyone over
  But you always thought, they will.

From Musgrave Street to Church Street
  A continuous milling throng,
There were Grandmas and young children
  And whole families strolling along,
Suddenly there'd be a hold up
  As the masses came to a stop,
Having spotted that weeks bargain
  In the window of a shop.

I liked going into Sages
  They sold all sorts of bits,
Every book you could imagine
  And those steel meccano kits,
If your parents had a club out
  Five pound it used to be,
A new hat for your mother
  And a toy for my brother and me.

We always called in Woolies
　With its bare and creaky floor,
And bought a lead soldier for sixpence
　Now that's what I call a store,
Curry's was quite famous
　As Lynn Streets coffee bar,
But not the place to be seen in
　Whilst with your Ma and Da.

And then there was the Market
　You could smell it from afar,
With every sweet you could think of
　In a packet or a jar,
You could sell old comics at some stalls
　And come away with money instead,
Then rushing back to Woolies toy counter
　For another soldier made of lead.

No parking fees in those days
　Few people owned a car,
You either travelled on public transport
　Or walked, no matter how far,
So all these people everywhere
　Out shopping to spend their pay,
And no better way of doing it
　Than in Lynn Street on a Saturday.

THE CINEMA (That never was)

I don't know when they built it
Or when they knocked it down,
But I always used to look at it
When on the bus from town.
I'd be upstairs on a double decker
Most were red but some were blue,
And as you passed under Throston bridge
The building came into view.
Futuristic in appearance
With that strangely looking face,
Supposedly built as a Cinema
Looking completely out of place.
I was usually fascinated
Wondering how it looked inside,
Had all the seats been fitted and
Would the screen be very wide.
Foreboding would describe it
Uninviting, bare and cold,
But then I suppose it would be
To a lad of ten years old.
It's gone like many other structures
Houses stand where it used to be,
For it never became a real Cinema
Showing Movies for people to see.

Years later I still had a question
I inquired of it's name, from someone,
He said "The building was called THE COMET"
And like a Comet, it's come and gone.

The Comet Cinema

BLUE BUSES

Now this could be a sensitive subject
So, I'd better explain from the start,
There used to be, Old and West Hartlepool
Although joined, but in many ways apart.

West Hartlepool ran all the buses
Painted a rather dark red,
But this was not deemed satisfactory
As some from Old Hartlepool, said.

So meetings were held and suggestions were made
And they finally decided what to do,
Old Hartlepool would have its own buses
But not painted red, they'd be blue.

The situation did cause a few problems
And the feelings of some were quite strong,
They'd stand at a bus stop for ages
Until one of the right colour came along.

But kids never bothered with politics
We always boarded one that was blue,
No allegiance was shown to either side
It was just, they were different and new.

But time proved a great persuader
Feelings mellowed and grew less strong,
When you needed a bus in a hurry
It mattered not which colour came along.

Now where did the blue buses go to
Having dropped their last passenger load,
They came all the way back to West Hartlepool
And parked up, just near Oxford Road.

The Blue Bus from the Old Side

TATTIE PICKEN

Pete kept repeating "Its ten bob a day"
"For pulling out potatoes, that's not bad pay",
We all just nodded and said he was right
But could we get up in the middle of the night?

It sounded so simple when sat in the class
Five days work, for a handful of brass,
The farm was near Elwick, so Pete had said
But the problem for me, would be getting out of bed.

The half term arrived, we were up with the lark
And all managed to meet at Ward Jackson Park,
Then fifty minutes later at a brisk walking rate
We came to the farm with its five barred gate.

Six hours later, I felt at deaths door
With a back that was breaking and a throat so sore,
Rain had pelted down for most of the day
I was soaking wet and knee deep in clay.

I'd met Pete and Mickey at the midday break
Mrs Farmer had given us some soup and a cake,
Mickey said "I've never worked so hard in me life"
"Back to work in five minutes" said the farmers wife.

We looked a sorry state, walking back into town
Covered in mud, each with his face in a frown,
Pete waved goodbye at his garden gate
"I'll see you in the morning and don't be late".

I had no recollection of getting into bed
With burning red cheeks and a wind blasted head,
It only seemed like minutes since I'd gone to sleep
Then off goes the alarm, with its bleep, bleep, bleep.

We lasted it out until Thursday night
I fell into bed and went out like a light,
Two pound I'd earned for those days of toil,
Drenched to the skin and covered in soil.

None of us made it back to the farm
Pete's good idea had lost its charm,
I laid in bed for most of the day
Then went down to Lynn Street to spend my pay.

SHOP AT BINNS

On every bus that drove round town
Those three words, I'd always see,
Stuck on the back, stuck on the front
"Shop at Binns", they said to me.

I didn't like that great big store
When I was just a little lad,
It seemed to go on for evermore
As I trailed behind my mam and dad.

I'd pull a face, then they'd get mad
And tell me to behave,
So I'd force a smile and catch them up
Oh, to be out of here, I'd crave.

Up to furniture, back down to clothes
It never seemed to stop,
What a way to spend Saturday
Traipsing round this shop.

By the time we got to the basement
I'd had my fill of the place,
And just about to kick up a fuss
Until seeing Mothers face.

Would you believe it, back up to hats
The three of us would go,
With mother trying hundreds on
As I walked to and fro.

I'd watch the lady at the till
Taking money from a shopper,
It was stuffed into a tube like thing
Then disappeared down a hopper.

Very strange it seemed to me
As to where the money went,
But a minute later the tube returned
From wherever it was sent.

The highlight of the day would come
When they took me down to toys,
Such a wondrous display met my eyes
And a section just for boys.

I'd gaze at the meccano sets
With their cogs and bolts and bars,
Imagining what could be made
Like diggers, trucks and cars.

The spell was broken, I'd got the call
My mam and dad were away,
With lifted spirits I wondered if
The shopping was done for the day.

I hurried then, with brisker step
To the first and then ground floor,
And had a smile upon my face
As I walked out through the door.

But happiness was alas, short lived
Defeated, I'd lost the cause,
As we headed off along Stockton Road
Towards the Central Stores.

I realise now, how wrong I was
That store was good for the town,
Like many things, not appreciated
Until they closed it down.

I remember a joke my father told
Putting on one of his grins,
"She was only a dustman's daughter
But she got her clothes from BINNS".

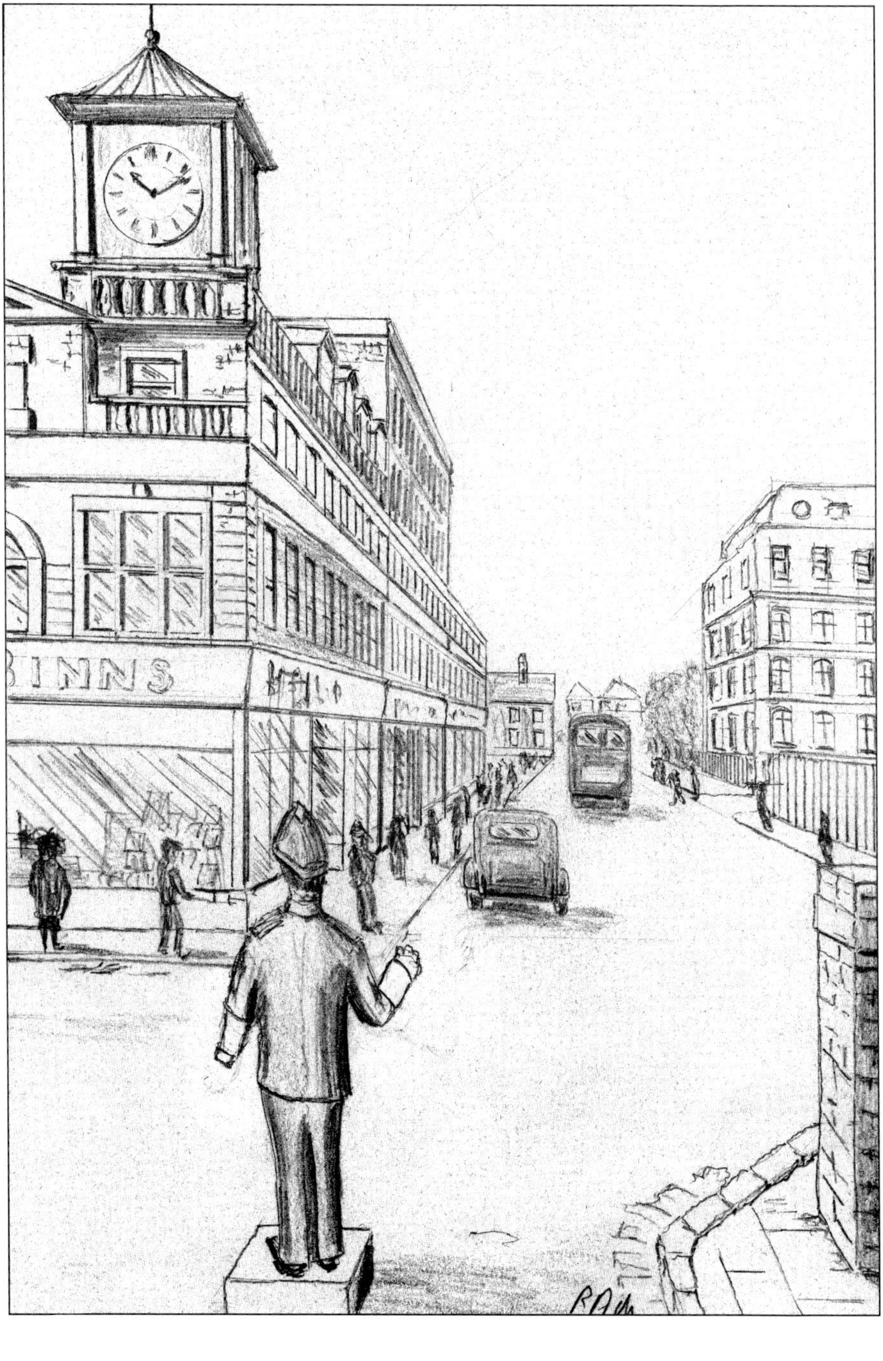
INNS

POLICEMAN AT BINNS CORNER

Do you remember that Bobby
And where he used to stand,
    His arms moved up
    His arms moved down
Like he was conducting a band.

On a little box he stood
He wore sleeves of cleanest white,
    He'd stop a bus here
    Wave on a car there
As he kept the traffic right.

I remember feeling quite nervous
As I pedalled along the road,
    Would I do the right thing
    Would I get it all wrong
Were his signals some kind of code.

It was over before I knew it
As he turned and faced my way,
    Then waving me on
    I pedalled like mad
That Bobby had made my day.

SIX OF THE BEST

The quickening heartbeat, the feeling of doom
Having been called up to the Headmaster's room,
Your mind playing havoc, for the wicked no rest
And hoping you're not for "six of the best".

The big door swings open, the form teachers there
He's stood to the right of the Headmasters chair,
Your mouth feels like sandpaper, Your tongue is dry too
As you realise the finger is pointed at you.

The charge is read out, your gaze hits the floor
Do you stand and take it, or run for the door,
Escape is no option, there's nowhere to go
As the cane suddenly appears, your mind says "Oh No".

Back to the classroom, all eyes gaze your way
They know what to look for, They've all had their day,
The lips that are quivering, the eyes that are red
They nod to each other, no words need be said.

The classroom is hushed as you sit at your place
With pulsating palms and a flush in your face,
Those thumping great heartbeats down in your chest
Just hoping that's the last time for "six of the best".

NOW POEMS

CLEVELAND COUNTY R.I.P.

Hartlepools on its own again
The chains are off at last,
We've broken free from Clevelands bands
Lets all together clap our hands,
Hip Hip Hooray.

We grind no axe with Teesside
Or Middlesbrough and the like,
We just prefer to have our say
And not by others miles away
Hip Hip Hooray.

It cost us dear to join that lot
All those years ago,
For quite a while they gave us pain
It's good to know we're out again,
Hip Hip Hooray.

Lets hope our leaders get it right
They owe it to the Town,
No more bureaucracy playing the fool
We need what's best for Hartlepool,
Hip Hip Hooray

Goodbye Cleveland, rest in peace
We wish you all the best,
No tears will fall, now that you're dead
And all split up and put to bed,
Hip Hip Hooray.

ELEPHANT ROCK

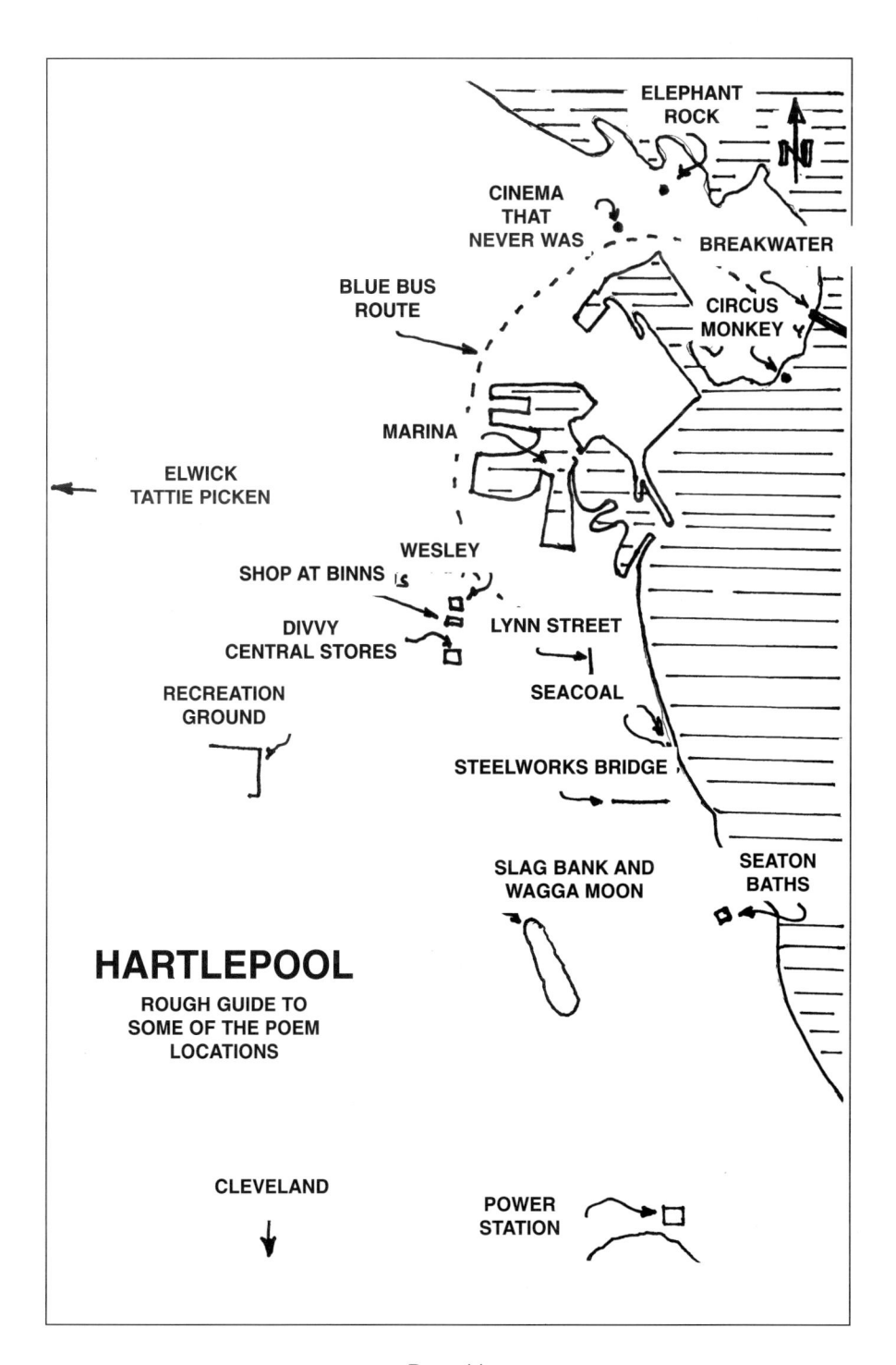

N

CINEMA THAT NEVER WAS

BREAKWATER

BLUE BUS ROUTE

CIRCUS MONKEY

MARINA

ELWICK TATTIE PICKEN

WESLEY

SHOP AT BINNS

DIVVY CENTRAL STORES

LYNN STREET

RECREATION GROUND

SEACOAL

STEELWORKS BRIDGE

SLAG BANK AND WAGGA MOON

SEATON BATHS

HARTLEPOOL
ROUGH GUIDE TO
SOME OF THE POEM
LOCATIONS

CLEVELAND

POWER STATION

IRON HORSE (Ridden by a 2000's Back Yard Hero)

When you don the leather jacket, the helmet, gloves and boots
And you sit astride that iron horse, it goes back to your roots,
As if your brain is telling you that all those years ago
Man chose a steed to ride on, as he travelled to and fro.

It's difficult to understand why a rider feels so free
When the visor's shut and the engine fires and it's just the bike and me,
It'll always be a mystery why some prefer two wheels
There is no answer logically, It's just the way one feels.

Now there's some prefer the British bikes, nostalgia I suppose
On the Bonnevilles, the Vincents and the Goldies they would pose,
Café racers were their names in nineteen sixty three
The epitome of independence to a biker just like me.

But now we're in 2000, technology is the name
With alloy frames and sixteen valves, It's the East that rules the game,
It's Kawasaki and It's Honda, Suzuki and the rest
If performance is required then the Japs they are the best.

So sitting on my G P X, from the land of the rising sun
And although I'm in my Fifties, I can still enjoy the fun,
Of cruising down the highway and doing what I like
And feeling very good to be, astride my Motorbike.

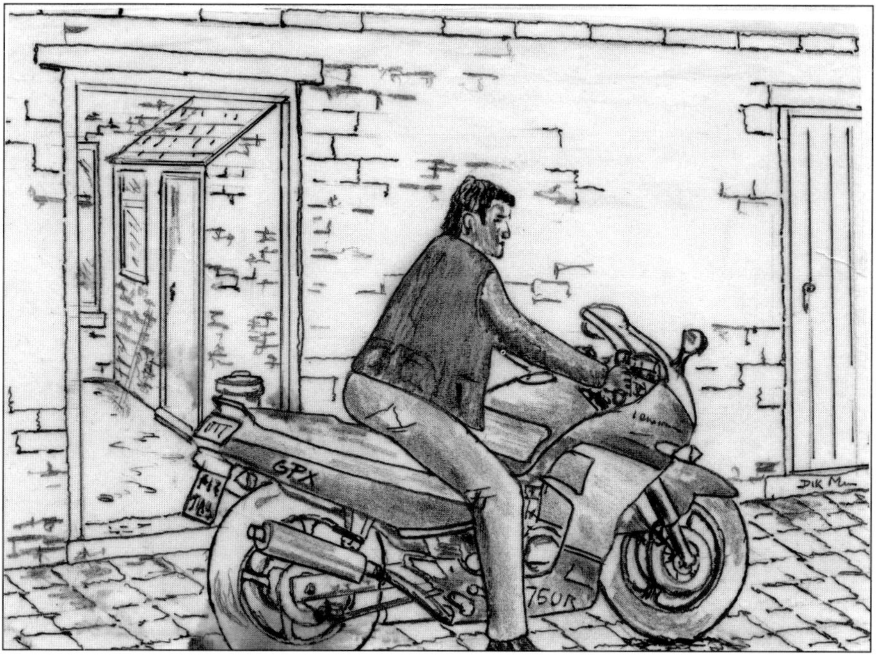
GPX
750R

EYE OF THE NIGHT

O, Wondrous orb of astral light
Shining, radiant in the night,
You borrow the rays, that come from our Sun
And shed them on Hartlepool, when night has begun.
You ball in the sky, You Eye of the Night
A glimpse of the Heavens, you give to our sight.

You appear in the dark and are gone in the day
Yet relentlessly travel in your own special way,
What power binds your terrible force
And controls your mass on Its orbital course.
With eyes of wonder we lift our gaze
And feast upon your nocturnal rays.

How long have you been there, looking at Earth
Silently, steadily encircling our girth,
Kingdoms have risen, the centuries have passed
You'll be there forever but kingdoms won't last.
O, Lunar sphere, you Lord of the Tide
Through corridors of Star Dust you ride and you ride.

O, Maker of moods, you Paladin of space
Rotating forever yet showing one face,
Presented to us from your place in the sky
We wonder, we wonder and ask ourselves why.
You ball in the sky, You Eye of the Night
What a Glimpse of the Heavens, you give to our sight.

What have you seen through these Eons of time
Have we tenants, violated this Mother of thine,
Are you disgusted with what we have done
To this God given planet that's warmed by the sun.
Ride on, Ride on, you Stallion of space
And keep on reflecting the light from your face.

As new dawn awakens your light fades away
Power decreasing with the advent of day,
El Sol now becomes master again
With searing light from its hydrogen brain.
Yet waiting in the wings for the sun to go down
You return in the night over Hartlepool Town.

O, Wondrous ball of astral light
With a visage that changes night after night,
We marvel at the power, that hung you in space
Does it kindle our Faith, does it generate Grace,
To accept there's a GOD much greater than we
Who set "THE EYE IN THE SKY" for humanity to see.

MILKMAN

Chink, Chink, ... Chink, Chink, Chink,
The sound that heralds the bottles of milk,
Delivered to our door, since I don't know when
Placed on the step by the early morning men.

Come winter, come summer, come hail, come shine
Every morning, the Chink and that electric cart whine,
How long it will last, no one can tell
For supermarkets are ringing the milkman's death knell.

Our milkman's named Vic, he's as sound as a pound
We live on the Fens which is part of his round,
Each friday afternoon he calls at our place
Collecting his money, a smile on his face.

Do you remember, in those days of old
And you went to the Co-op, where tokens were sold,
Put under the empties last thing at night
And replaced with fresh pints as the day became light.

And what about those bottles when I was a kid
With a round cardboard disc, stuck in as a lid,
The Girls saved the tops, it seemed the done thing
Then hung round their necks on a piece of string.

I know it costs more when milk comes this way
And budgets need meeting at the end of the day,
But I'll get it delivered as long as I can
By that early morning all weather friendly Milkman.

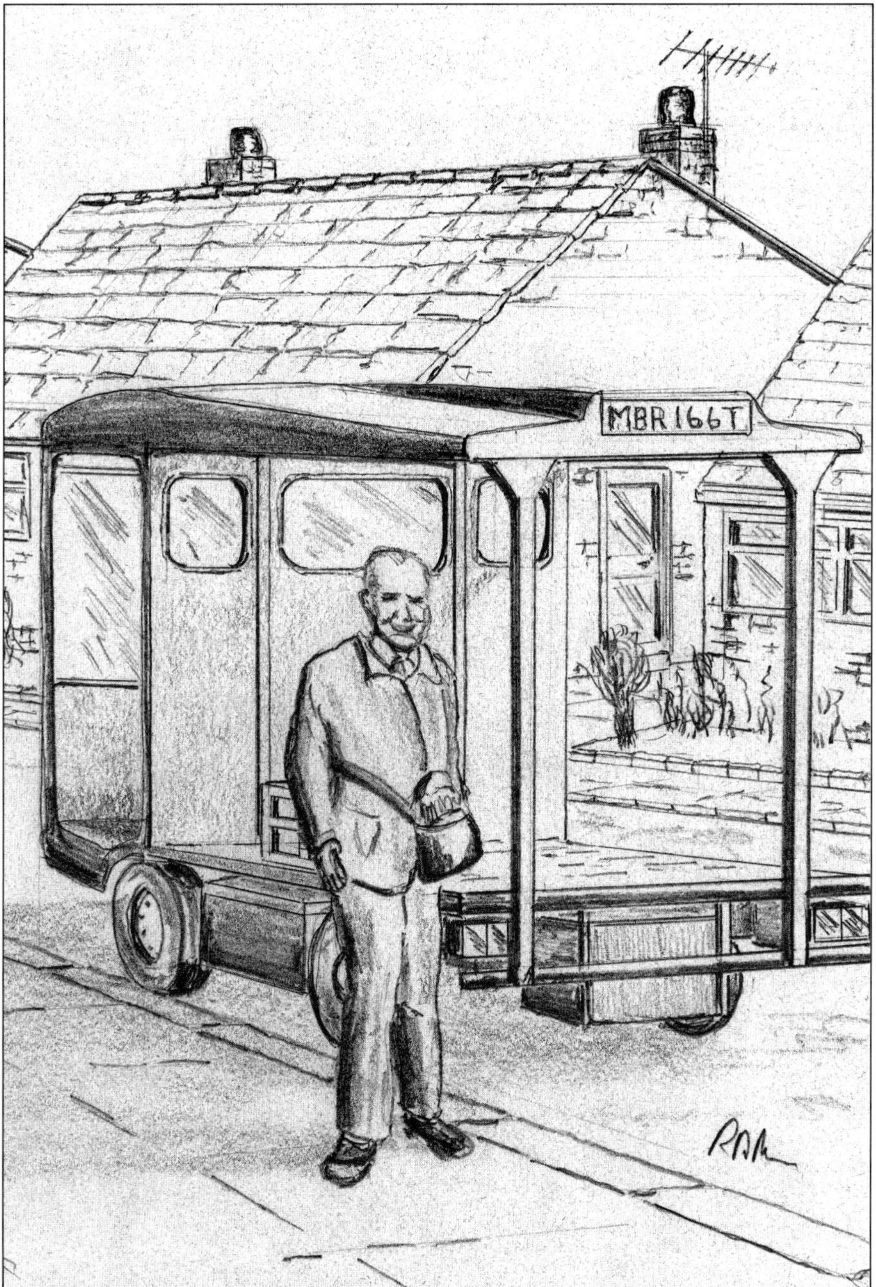
MBR166T

ODE TO CABLE T.V.

The attack comes every morning
As the sunlight paints the skies,
In pick-up trucks and transit vans
The Warriors swarm like flies.

Have these men come for battle
As they spread out round the town,
In teams of four and teams of five
Their bodies fit, their faces brown.

They do not carry weapons
Likes guns or sharpened blades,
The arms that these men bring along
Are shovels, picks and spades.

So who, perchance is the enemy
Of this mobile Motley Crew,
Have they come to vent their anger
On the likes of me and the likes of you.

Fear not, O gentle resident
Don't worry I implore,
This conflict rages on the Streets
You're safe behind your door.

Well done O patient reader
Those clues you've twigged at last,
The cause of this trench warfare
Is a company named Comcast.

Yes the town is getting Cabled
With a thirty channel T.V.
So every couch potato
Can get glued to their settee.

So what about the lads that dig
To make this dream come true,
They work non stop for hour on end
To lay a cable for me and you.

Top marks must go to these workers
Who so often collect the blame,
For broken drives and holes in the roads
Plus the odd insurance claim.

We hear the still saw whining
And the drone of the big crane truck,
That drives around between the teams
Delivering things and collecting the muck.

And although you're safe behind your door
Don't venture out on the road,
For the drivers of these vehicles
Have never heard of the Highway Code.

But when the work is over
And the dust has settled down,
Will you miss this roadside army
Who came to attack your town.

There is one thought, however
Will put a smile upon your face,
As the Warriors leave your doorstep
They're attacking another place.

THE OLD MAN AND THE BREAKWATER

Upon a seat at Hartlepool front
Each day I come and ponder,
I stare at the Sea, then my gaze is fixed
On the Breakwater over yonder.

Like some gigantic finger of stone
Pointing away from the land,
Laid there to battle natures might
Built straight by human hand.

A certain sadness fills my thoughts
Remembering what used to be,
When crowds of people walked each day
Along the Breakwater, out to sea.

I remember being a fit young man
In nineteen forty five,
With a little boat and lobster pots
So strong and so alive.

Out in my boat, off Hartlepool front
Laying those pots in the sea,
And waving at people on the Breakwater
As they called and waved at me.

Any day of the week they'd be there
Those men with rod and reel,
Hoping to take home to the family
A freshly caught fishy meal.

Then all those courting couples
Out walking hand in hand,
They'd stop and lean on the handrail
And look back to the land.

The parents and their children
Enjoying a sunday walk,
That finger of stone was alive then
With laughter and peoples talk.

The Sky turns grey and I feel cold
The wind brings the smell of the sea,
I'm back in my boat off Hartlepool front
So young and oh, so free.

I'd like to sit here longer
But I've suddenly lost the will,
For the wind is bringing rain now
And I shiver against its chill.

So slowly I return to the hostel
Having turned my back to the sea,
My thoughts are of warmth and comfort
Just waiting to welcome me.

I stop once on my journey
And turning, look back again
Across at the old Breakwater
Now battered by wind and rain.

We both are old and weathered
Worn down by time and tide,
Yet I know you'll still be out there
When this old man has died.

MARINA

What a change has taken place
In this town where we reside
We've seen the unemployment
And those Industries that died
Yet like the mythical Phoenix
Rising from the fire and strife
Hartlepool is alive again
It's breathing with new life.

Take a look around the Marina
And what's been done so far
You'll see it best by walking
So park and leave the car
It's really hard to imagine
What the place looked like before
With all these alterations
Just a stones throw from the shore.

For now there's families living
Where the coal staiths used to be
In modern flats and houses
With views towards the sea
The dock is full of boats again
Where the Warrior used to lay
But it's mainly used for leisure
Now shipbuilding's had its day.

Spend some time at the lock gates
It's an interesting place to be
As sailing boats and fishermen
Venture out towards the sea
The raising of the sailcloth
Of ropes and swaying mast
It brings to life our heritage
And memories of the past.

The Historic Quay is amazing
As you walk through days of old
The sights and sounds of yesterday
And the story they unfold
The Wingfield Castle and Trincomalee
Restored with skillful hands
These boats that spent their working life
In those far and distant lands.

So sceptics eat your hearts out
And cynics just like me
Who didn't think we'd ever get
Our Marina by the sea
It's taken years to get there
But worth it you'll agree
For helping with the rebirth
Of this Town beside the sea.

GROWING OLD IN HARTLEPOOL

Creak, Creak, go the joints
In your arms your legs and neck,
What's the cause of all this pain
The cause is age, O flipping heck.

The summers come, the summers go
Another birthday comes around,
The bounce has gone, you start to shrink
Your head gets nearer to the ground.

If these few problems ended here
It wouldn't really be so bad,
But the body still would like to do
The things it did, when still a lad.

I'm in a mid way generation
Between the young and very old,
No more hassle, things run smooth
A happy time, or so I'm told.

Look forward to the future
Positive thinking is the way,
Keep working, working, working
Until retirement day.

Then a whole new world will open
With these benefits, it's been said,
Incontinence pills, the walking stick
And an orthopaedic bed.

But lets look on the bright side
Growing old can be just fine,
Face each new day as a bonus
Like the last of the summer wine.

Creak, Creak, Creak.

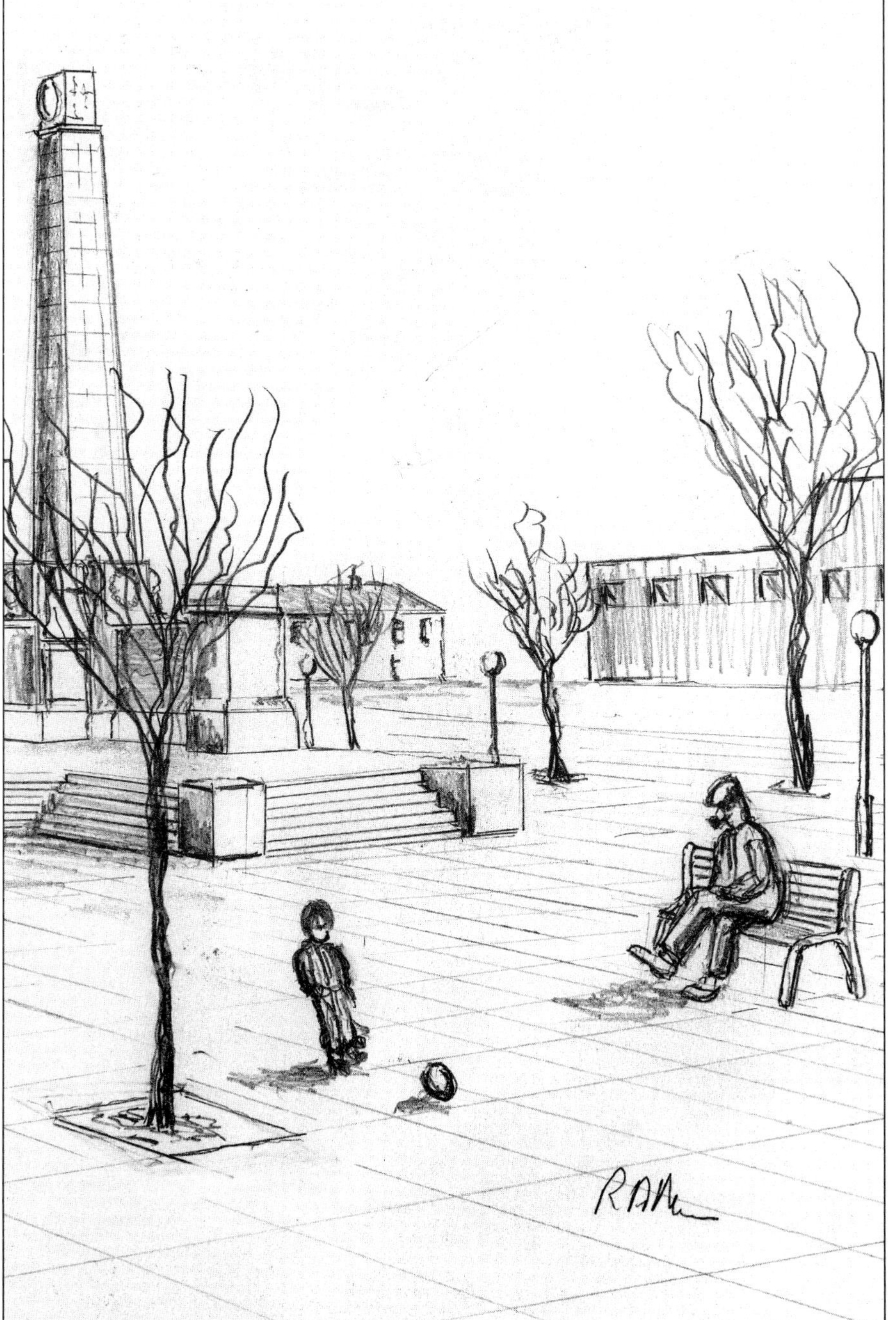

THE WESLEY (A MOUSE'S TALE)

My Great, Great, Great, Great Grandfather
Or so the story's told
Lived within these very walls
In those days of old,
He was a noble Chieftain
My father told me that
He ruled the mice for many years
Until eaten by a cat

The Wesley was a house of peace
In those bygone days
With sounds of people praying
And searching for God's ways,
Sunday they'd come marching in
Then the music would start to play
The building filled with singing
As they praised their maker's day.

My Great, Great, Great Grandfather
Saw changes taking place
The people stopped coming
No more a human face,
Where feet once trod, now only paws
Disturbed the dust of time
Then the pigeons came and added to
The dirt, decay and grime.

My father was a Chieftain
Just like that one of old
He ruled the mice of the Wesley
In a building of dark and cold,
I remember last seeing my father
As I heard that awful slap
He lay quite still with broken neck
Upon a cheese filled trap.

Yes, people had returned again
To this dark abandoned place
But different sounds came with them
No songs of "Amazing Grace",
Great rumbling and disturbance
And death for many a mouse
As they chopped and changed the inside
Of this old and special house.

I am now a Chieftain
And the mice ask this of me
What do we do?. Where can we go?
They'll kill us all, you'll see,
The Wesley's now a nightclub
With people back again
The poison's down, the traps are set
Our life is full of pain.

My son is now the Chieftain
For I am old and grey
Our clan is few in numbers
Unlike my Grandfather's day,
The Wesley's not our home how
We've left our old abode
Bags were packed and off we marched
To the Grand across the road.

       Squeak, Squeak, Squeak

ON THE DOLE, AGAIN

I'm here again in Victoria Road
Then up three flights of stairs
Trying to get employment
With all its woes and cares
Getting back to work, it says
On the signs all over the place
Then a look at what's on offer
Wipes the smile right off your face.

Poor Hartlepool's sited wrongly
Towards the top end of the map
We're on a loser straight away
Being north of the Watford Gap
When it comes to unemployment
This is the place to be
Three hundred miles from London
Beside the cold North Sea.

So I make a determined effort
And look at the jobs on show
There's one pay's over a hundred pound
But to Bristol, I'd have to go
There's temporary this and part-time that
It's enough to make you moan
Security Guards wanted urgently
Must have, a car, a dog and a phone.

The staff indeed are helpful
But there's not much they can do
With all these people out of work
And vacant posts, so few
I'm not asking for the earth
Just the chance to earn a few bob
But I'm back again in Victoria Road
Having failed to get a job.

But let's look on the bright side
I'll call back another day
Maybe then I'll find a job
With fairly decent pay
And I'll buy the local papers
Seeking jobs will be my goal
Cos, if I'm out of work for six months
They're going to stop my dole.

POWER STATION

Nigh on thirty years it's stood there
A few miles south east of the town,
It was back in nineteen sixty eight
When the foundations were laid down.

Like some gigantic breeze block
When you view it from afar,
For most folk only see it
Through the window of a car.

Thousands of men worked on that site
During the construction stage,
They came from all over the country
With the promise of a decent wage.

Locals too, have had their share
Of jobs and general trade,
There's quite a lot within the plant
We know is Hartlepool made.

Its producing loads of electricity
Thousands of megawatts a day,
Sending out all that energy
As the station pays its way.

Nuclear energy is on our doorstep
Whether we like it or we don't,
There's those who accept atomic power
But there's always some that won't.

Yet the station could be in danger
It's competitors gathering en-mass,
For they are producing electricity
By burning North Sea gas.

So its future could be troubled
By others in the energy race,
But no one knows the answer
It's a case of, watch this space.

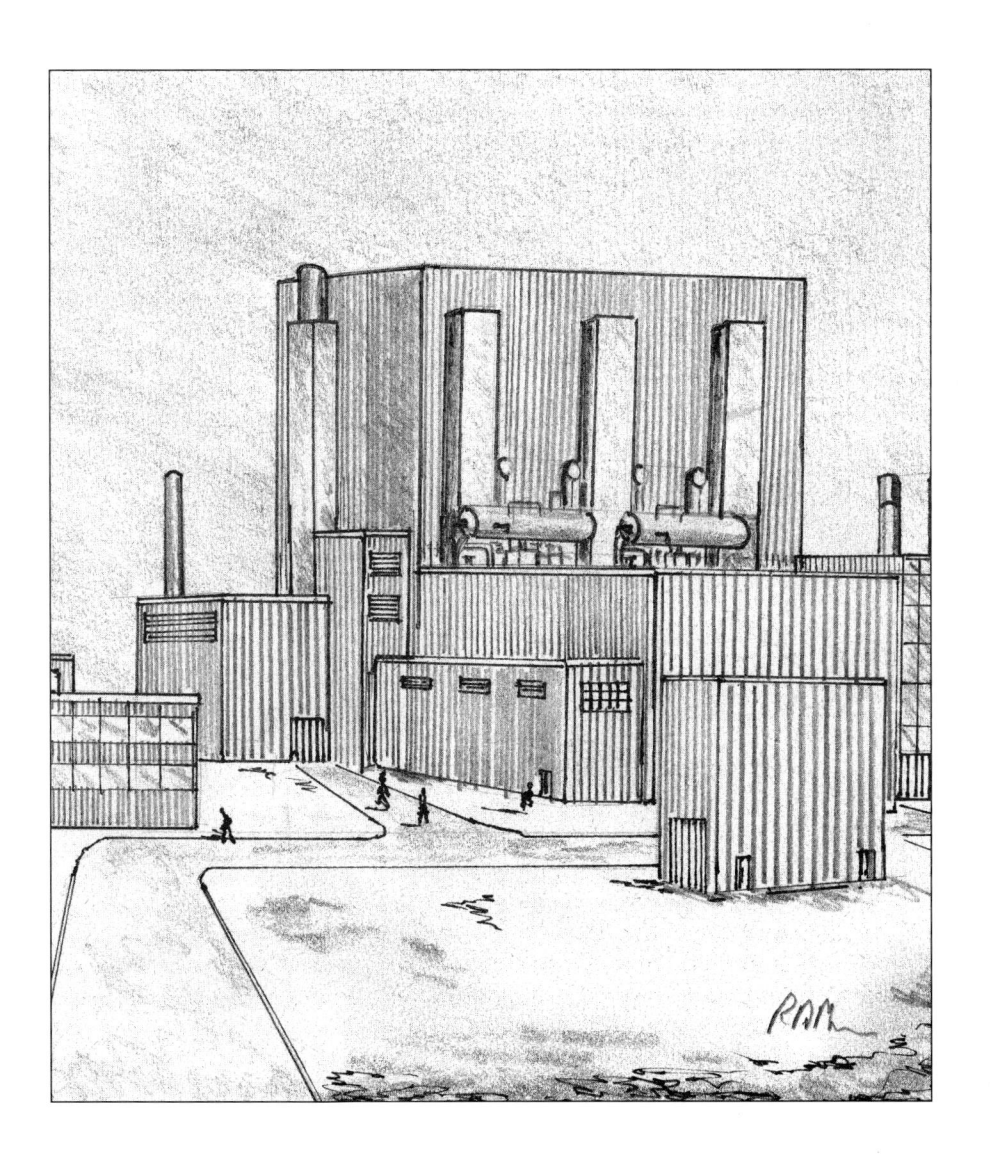
RAM

SEAGULLS

They don't look all that big
When soaring in the sky,
Forever noisy in their flight
That haunting wailing cry.
But if one flies above your head
Or lands close to your side,
Its amazing how big they are
With wing so very wide.

They sometimes fly across the land
When tide and wind decree,
And settle in some grassy field
As a respite from the sea,
Then glide above your garden
In circles o so wide,
Just waiting for the signal
From the wind and changing tide.

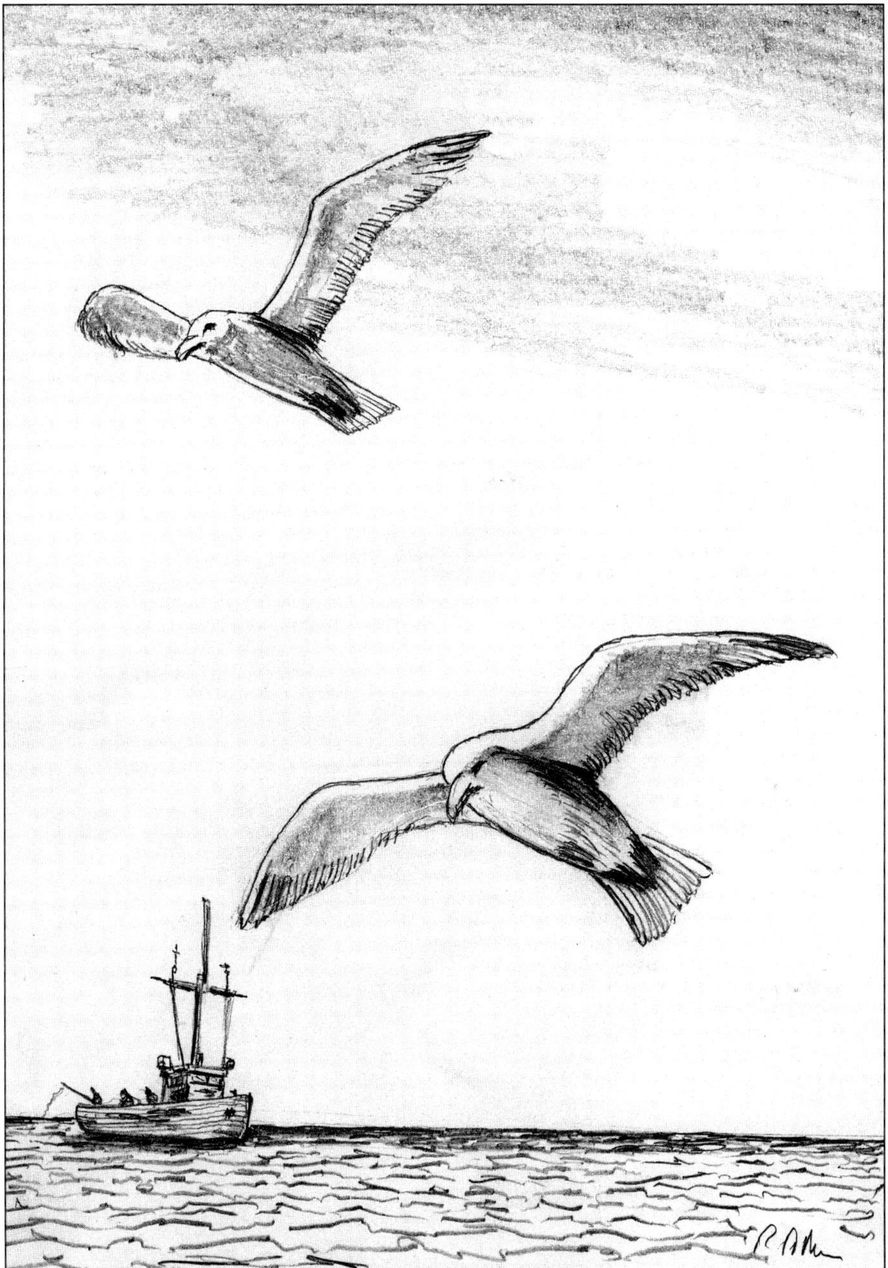

WHATEVER HAPPENED TO SUNDAY

A day of peace
A day of rest,
The Sundays of old
Were really the best.

The old week over
A time to reflect,
To recharge your batteries
And thoughts to collect.

Sunday has gone now
It's just another day,
Most shops are open
To take away your pay.

Supermarkets, Hyperstores
Shopping malls too,
They're only too willing
To look after you.

Do we have time
To think about life,
Among all the bustle
Amidst all the strife.

Life seems such a rush
No time to spare,
You need to be here
They want you to be there.

Sunday was a brake
For body and mind,
It calmed you down
It helped you unwind.

Will they come back
Those days of before,
Unfortunately not
We'll see them no more.

It's really a pity
It's really a shame,
That Sunday's still Sunday
But only in name.

STEELWORKS BRIDGE

Prologue

Such a proud pedestrian highway
Standing on stilts of steel
Heading towards the seaside
Trodden on, by many a heel,
    Its course was straight, Its frame was strong
    For many years people passed along.

Kids ran along that highway
As they headed towards the sand
For a days adventure at Seaton
Away from the streets and the land
Sometimes mother was with them
Shouting "Don't get too far ahead"
She'd be loaded down with a picnic
Lemonade, cups and brown bread.

And then the weary workmen
At all times of the day
Heading for Mainsforth Terrace
Clocking on to earn their pay
Hearing the roar of the furnace
Watching the molten steel
The heat and the sparks of the North Works
In a world that was so unreal.

As you walked along that highway
Dodging the gaps between your feet
Looking down on a world of Industry
Catching the smells and feeling the heat
Suddenly a train would pass under
Belching hot steam all around
Then your world would become rather hazy
Fading the light and dulling the sound.

But what a change of vista
As you continued on your way
With sights of the works behind you
Replaced by views of Seaton Bay
That bridge was a spanning of contrasts
Uniting the town and the sea
Nothing special, just taken for granted
By a local lad like me.

Epilogue

Such a proud pedestrian highway
One section still remains
It stands above the railway lines
That now carry the diesel trains
      Its course was straight, Its frame was strong
      For many years people passed along.

RUBBISH

What on earth's a Midden, I can hear you say
Well, some will remember that bygone day,
When rubbish and ashes and papers and all
Where tipped in the backyard in a hole in the wall.
Then once a week the men came along
To clear out your midden and get rid of the pong
It was pulled out its hole and dumped in the truck
And all ended up with the rest of the muck.

The dustbin arrived as the years moved along
A receptacle of steel and really quite strong,
The man would collect it from outside your place,
Then return it all empty, a smile on his face.
The bin would last for a number of years
With the odd bit of maintenance and minor repairs,
But time and the weather would have their day
And the bottom of your bin would rust away.

Black plastic bags were the next in line
No more coal fires, so that was fine.
You had to place them on the side of the road
Which made it easier for the binman to load.
The council provided bags that were left at your door
If you made too much rubbish you had to buy more.
It seemed like the bags were here to stay,
But time marches on and they've had their day.

The bags, the dustbins, the middens all gone
And a new contraption is now number one.
It arrived one day and entered our scene
Big and green and spotlessly clean.
The wheelie bins here and seems just fine,
Environmentally coloured and the latest design.
So fill up those containers with whatever you can,
And leave it near the road for the refuse man.

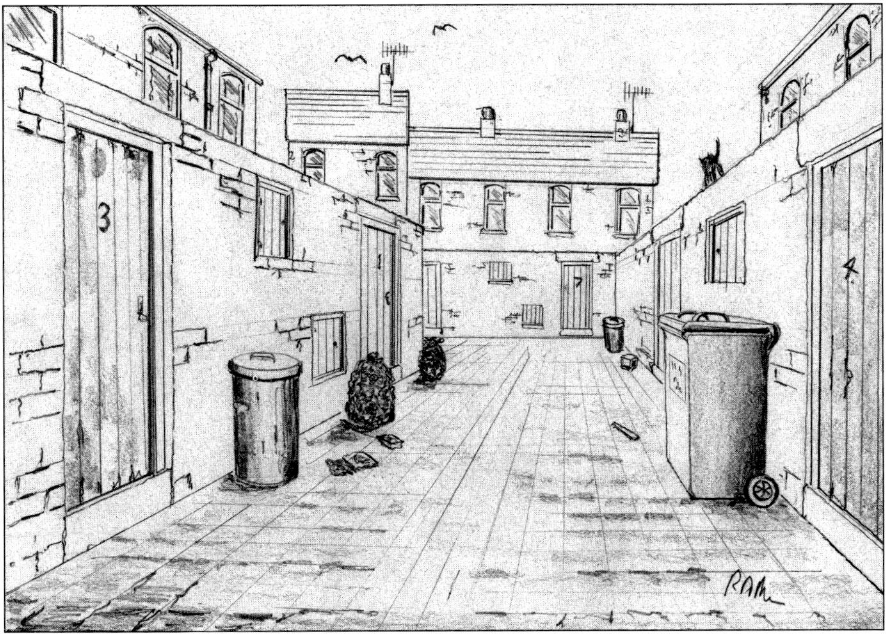
3
7
4

NOTES